Sorting

Karina Law

SEA-TO-SEA

Mankato Collingwood London

Contents

Look for Tiger on the pages of this book. Sometimes he is hiding.

Every day we sort things in different ways.

food

paper

cars

coins

jigsaw pieces

3

Sorting Shapes

We sort things into groups.

I am sorting different shapes.

round

straight

5

Laundry Day

Anya, Ed, and Felix are helping
to sort the laundry.

6

We sort the dry clothes and put them away. They will be easy to find.

I am sorting these socks into pairs. Can you find an odd sock?

7

Tidy Up Time!

Mom asks Harrison, Billy, and Mira to tidy up.

Harrison! Billy! Tidy up your books please.

Mira, tidy up the plates please.

Tidy up these groups! Can you spot the odd one in each group?

9

Many and Few

Here are many cars.

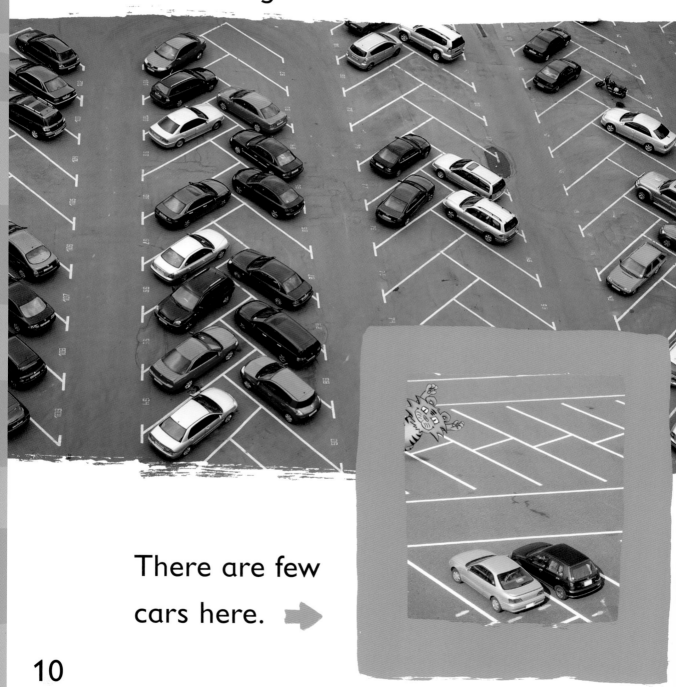

There are few cars here. ➡

Here are many masks.

There are few
masks here. ➡

Which is your
favorite mask?

Sorting Materials

Lola is sorting materials for recycling.

1

Felix is sorting recycled materials to make a robot.

2

He needs tubes for the arms and the legs. He covers paper towel tubes in foil. They will be the arms.

Felix cuts another tube in half. He makes the two pieces into legs and covers them with foil.

Next, he cuts out decorations for his robot.

Then Felix sticks on the decorations. His robot is almost finished.

He makes a robot head. Now his recycled robot is ready for action!

15

Dinner Time!

Carlo and Anya are setting the table for dinner. There will be four people.

Carlo sorts out the knives and forks.

Anya sorts out the glasses and plates.

How many plates does she need?

Are there enough glasses?

Fair Sorting

Felix and Ed sort out the fruit.
Everyone has the same amount.

Lola pours the juice.

Everyone has the same amount. Now the pitcher is empty.

Now what has happened? Does everyone have the same?

Sorting Shopping

Store shelves are sorted into rows.

At home, Lola sorts out the bottles and boxes.

Carlo is sorting some coins.

I have sorted the coins.

Help Anya to sort these into two groups: fruit and vegetables.

broccoli

banana

apple

orange

pear

papaya

carrot

apricot

beans

21

Make a Sorting Box

1 Jenna is making a sorting box.

She gets an empty box.

2

She cuts out some strips of thin cardboard.

3

Then Jenna glues the strips into the box.

4 Now she can use it to sort out her pens, pencils, and crayons.

How could you decorate your sorting box?

Word Picture Bank

Masks—page 11

Recycling—page 12

Robot—pages 13, 14, 15

Shelves—page 20

Tidy up—pages 8, 9

Laundry—page 6, 7

This edition first published in 2011 by
Sea-to-Sea Publications
Distributed by Black Rabbit Books
P.O. Box 3263, Mankato, Minnesota 56002
Copyright © Sea-to-Sea Publications 2011
Printed in China, Dongguan
All rights reserved.

Library of Congress Cataloging-in-Publication Data
Law, Karina.
 Sorting / by Karina Law.
    p. cm. -- (Tiger talk. Number fun)
 Summary: "Provides young readers with an introduction to the concept of
sorting and describes how this skill is used in their daily life"--Provided by
publisher.
 ISBN 978-1-59771-258-3 (lib. bd.)
1. Set theory--Juvenile literature. 2. Group theory--Juvenile literature. I.
Title.
 QA174.5.L39 2011
 511.3'22--dc22
                                        2009052668

9 8 7 6 5 4 3 2

Published by arrangement with the Watts Publishing Group Ltd, London.

Series editor: Adrian Cole
Photographer: Andy Crawford (unless otherwise credited)
Design: Sphere Design Associates
Art director: Jonathan Hair
Acknowledgments: The Publisher would like to thank Norrie Carr model agency. "Tiger"
and "Rabbit" puppets used with kind permission from Ravensden PLC
(www.ravensden.co.uk). Tiger Talk logo drawn by Kevin Hopgood. Picture Credits:
Ronen/Shutterstock: 7t and 24cr (clothes). WizData Inc/Shutterstock: 11, 24tl. Norman
Pogson/Shutterstock: 10b. Nicholas Sutcliffe/Shutterstock: 3br. J. Helgason/Shutterstock: 9bl.
Andrey Khrolenok/Shutterstock: 10t. Vasiliy Koval/Shutterstock: 3bl. Edyta Pawlowska/
Shutterstock: 3tr. Dusty Cline/Shutterstock: 9t. Andriy Rovenko/Shutterstock: 20t, 24cl. Vincent
Giordano/Shutterstock: 9c (car). Nadezda/Shutterstock: 9bc. Silvano Audisio/Shutterstock:
3lc. Elena Schweitzer/
Shutterstock: 9bc (brick). Stillfx/Shutterstock: 3tc.
Obak/Shutterstock: 9b (big bear).
Quaxelc/Shutterstock: 9cr.
Dori O'Connell/iStockphoto: 8b, 24bc.
Every attempt has been made to clear
copyright. Should there be any
inadvertent omission please apply
to the publisher for rectification.

March 2010
RD/6000006414/002

There are 18 Tigers, including me, in this book. Did you find all of us?